Name

Wishes and Comments

Name

Wishes and Comments

Name

Wishes and Comments

Name

Wishes and Comments

Name | Wishes and Comments

Name | Wishes and Comments

Name | Wishes and Comments

Name | Wishes and Comments

Name

Wishes and Comments

Name

Wishes and Comments

Name

Wishes and Comments

Name

Wishes and Comments

Name

Wishes and Comments

Name

Wishes and Comments

Name

Wishes and Comments

Name

Wishes and Comments

Name

Wishes and Comments

Name

Wishes and Comments

Name

Wishes and Comments

Name

Wishes and Comments

Name | Wishes and Comments

Name | Wishes and Comments

Name | Wishes and Comments

Name | Wishes and Comments

Name Wishes and Comments

Name Wishes and Comments

Name Wishes and Comments

Name Wishes and Comments

Name

Wishes and Comments

Name

Wishes and Comments

Name

Wishes and Comments

Name

Wishes and Comments

Name Wishes and Comments

Name Wishes and Comments

Name Wishes and Comments

Name Wishes and Comments

Name

Wishes and Comments

Name

Wishes and Comments

Name

Wishes and Comments

Name

Wishes and Comments

Name

Wishes and Comments

Name

Wishes and Comments

Name

Wishes and Comments

Name

Wishes and Comments

Name

Wishes and Comments

Name

Wishes and Comments

Name

Wishes and Comments

Name

Wishes and Comments

Name

Wishes and Comments

Name

Wishes and Comments

Name

Wishes and Comments

Name

Wishes and Comments

Name

Wishes and Comments

Name

Wishes and Comments

Name

Wishes and Comments

Name

Wishes and Comments

Name | Wishes and Comments

Name | Wishes and Comments

Name | Wishes and Comments

Name | Wishes and Comments

Name Wishes and Comments

Name Wishes and Comments

Name Wishes and Comments

Name Wishes and Comments

Name

Wishes and Comments

Name

Wishes and Comments

Name

Wishes and Comments

Name

Wishes and Comments

Name Wishes and Comments

Name Wishes and Comments

Name Wishes and Comments

Name Wishes and Comments

Name | Wishes and Comments

Name | Wishes and Comments

Name | Wishes and Comments

Name | Wishes and Comments

Name

Wishes and Comments

Name

Wishes and Comments

Name

Wishes and Comments

Name

Wishes and Comments

Name

Wishes and Comments

Name

Wishes and Comments

Name

Wishes and Comments

Name

Wishes and Comments

Name | Wishes and Comments

Name | Wishes and Comments

Name | Wishes and Comments

Name | Wishes and Comments

Name Wishes and Comments

Name Wishes and Comments

Name Wishes and Comments

Name Wishes and Comments

Name | Wishes and Comments

Name | Wishes and Comments

Name | Wishes and Comments

Name | Wishes and Comments

Name

Wishes and Comments

Name

Wishes and Comments

Name

Wishes and Comments

Name

Wishes and Comments

Name | Wishes and Comments

Name | Wishes and Comments

Name | Wishes and Comments

Name | Wishes and Comments

Name

Wishes and Comments

Name

Wishes and Comments

Name

Wishes and Comments

Name

Wishes and Comments

Name | Wishes and Comments

Name | Wishes and Comments

Name | Wishes and Comments

Name | Wishes and Comments

Name Wishes and Comments

Name Wishes and Comments

Name Wishes and Comments

Name Wishes and Comments

Name

Wishes and Comments

Name

Wishes and Comments

Name

Wishes and Comments

Name

Wishes and Comments

Name

Wishes and Comments

Name

Wishes and Comments

Name

Wishes and Comments

Name

Wishes and Comments

Name Wishes and Comments

Name Wishes and Comments

Name Wishes and Comments

Name Wishes and Comments

Name Wishes and Comments

Name Wishes and Comments

Name Wishes and Comments

Name Wishes and Comments

Name

Wishes and Comments

Name

Wishes and Comments

Name

Wishes and Comments

Name

Wishes and Comments

Name Wishes and Comments

Name Wishes and Comments

Name Wishes and Comments

Name Wishes and Comments

Name Wishes and Comments

Name Wishes and Comments

Name Wishes and Comments

Name Wishes and Comments

Name

Wishes and Comments

Name

Wishes and Comments

Name

Wishes and Comments

Name

Wishes and Comments

Name

Wishes and Comments

Name

Wishes and Comments

Name

Wishes and Comments

Name

Wishes and Comments

Name | Wishes and Comments

Name | Wishes and Comments

Name | Wishes and Comments

Name | Wishes and Comments

Name | Wishes and Comments

Name | Wishes and Comments

Name | Wishes and Comments

Name | Wishes and Comments

Name | Wishes and Comments

Name | Wishes and Comments

Name | Wishes and Comments

Name | Wishes and Comments

Name

Wishes and Comments

Name

Wishes and Comments

Name

Wishes and Comments

Name

Wishes and Comments

Name

Wishes and Comments

Name

Wishes and Comments

Name

Wishes and Comments

Name

Wishes and Comments

Name

Wishes and Comments

Name

Wishes and Comments

Name

Wishes and Comments

Name

Wishes and Comments

Name

Wishes and Comments

Name

Wishes and Comments

Name

Wishes and Comments

Name

Wishes and Comments

Name

Wishes and Comments

Name

Wishes and Comments

Name

Wishes and Comments

Name

Wishes and Comments

Name

Wishes and Comments

Name

Wishes and Comments

Name

Wishes and Comments

Name

Wishes and Comments

Name | Wishes and Comments
Name | Wishes and Comments
Name | Wishes and Comments
Name | Wishes and Comments

Name

Wishes and Comments

Name

Wishes and Comments

Name

Wishes and Comments

Name

Wishes and Comments

Name

Wishes and Comments

Name

Wishes and Comments

Name

Wishes and Comments

Name

Wishes and Comments

Name

Wishes and Comments

Name

Wishes and Comments

Name

Wishes and Comments

Name

Wishes and Comments

Name | Wishes and Comments

Name | Wishes and Comments

Name | Wishes and Comments

Name | Wishes and Comments

Name Wishes and Comments

Name Wishes and Comments

Name Wishes and Comments

Name Wishes and Comments

Name Wishes and Comments

Name Wishes and Comments

Name Wishes and Comments

Name Wishes and Comments

Name

Wishes and Comments

Name

Wishes and Comments

Name

Wishes and Comments

Name

Wishes and Comments

Name | Wishes and Comments

Name | Wishes and Comments

Name | Wishes and Comments

Name | Wishes and Comments

Name

Wishes and Comments

Name

Wishes and Comments

Name

Wishes and Comments

Name

Wishes and Comments

Name

Wishes and Comments

Name

Wishes and Comments

Name

Wishes and Comments

Name

Wishes and Comments

Name

Wishes and Comments

Name

Wishes and Comments

Name

Wishes and Comments

Name

Wishes and Comments

Name Wishes and Comments

Name Wishes and Comments

Name Wishes and Comments

Name Wishes and Comments

Name | Wishes and Comments

Name | Wishes and Comments

Name | Wishes and Comments

Name | Wishes and Comments

Name Wishes and Comments

Name Wishes and Comments

Name Wishes and Comments

Name Wishes and Comments

Name

Wishes and Comments

Name

Wishes and Comments

Name

Wishes and Comments

Name

Wishes and Comments

Name

Wishes and Comments

Name

Wishes and Comments

Name

Wishes and Comments

Name

Wishes and Comments

Name Wishes and Comments

Name Wishes and Comments

Name Wishes and Comments

Name Wishes and Comments

Name

Wishes and Comments

Name

Wishes and Comments

Name

Wishes and Comments

Name

Wishes and Comments

Name Wishes and Comments

Name Wishes and Comments

Name Wishes and Comments

Name Wishes and Comments

Name

Wishes and Comments

Name

Wishes and Comments

Name

Wishes and Comments

Name

Wishes and Comments

Name | Wishes and Comments

Name | Wishes and Comments

Name | Wishes and Comments

Name | Wishes and Comments

www.ingramcontent.com/pod-product-compliance
Lightning Source LLC
Chambersburg PA
CBHW061749260326
41914CB00006B/1035
9781839903199